THE CONJURER

Pedro Serrano
THE CONJURER

Translated from the Spanish
& introduced by
Anna Crowe

2024

Published by Arc Publications,
Nanholme Mill, Shaw Wood Road,
Todmorden OL14 6DA, UK
www.arcpublications.co.uk

978 1911469 78 0

Design by Tony Ward
Printed in the UK by
TJ Books, Padstow, Cornwall

COVER
Detail from
'Mimetisme', 2015, © Alan Glass 2024 (artist's collection).
Lithography, mounted and assembled insects, wood, plastic,
and dry branches in a wooden box, 181 x 24 x 16 cm.
By kind permission of the artist.
Cover photograph: © Gerardo Landa / Eduardo López, 2024

ACKNOWLEDGEMENTS
'Clinamen' was published by *The High Window* in 2018;
'Archimedes' Elephant' was published by the Bitter Oleander
Press in 2020; 'Frost in Auxonne' was published by *Another
Chicago Magazine* in 2020

Arc Translations Series
Series Editor: Jean Boase-Beier

CONTENTS

Introduction / 8

Arc's second volume of poems by Pedro Serrano, draws on both unpublished and published work from his collections, *Desplazamientos, Nueces,* and *Lo que falta.* Co-author of *La Generación del Cordero* (Trilce Ediciones, 2000), an anthology of contemporary British and Irish poetry, Serrano here takes his place among his companions in poetry, poets like Don Paterson, Kathleen Jamie, the late Matthew Sweeney, W. N. Herbert, Richard Gwyn, the late John Burnside, Jamie McKendrick and the late Sarah Maguire, among others. Passionate and full of music, these poems explore the natural world with its wonders, and confront the passing of time, decay and change. He demands that we 'take note of the slippage of all that is real in a poem. That is to say, what the language of a poem succeeds in bringing about is a shift away from the rigid categories of meaning, where the world is on one side and language on the other, into a space in which all that is real comes across. The poem allows us to speak to the world, the world understood in its broadest sense, that is, for example, the voice and movement of birds, but of also the constellations in the sky, of the chemical processes within the human body, of the weight of the ocean's tides. Here I am not sublimating the power of the poem, but on the contrary, allowing it to settle and become calm and thus allow us to see what it is capable of doing. But that has always been the métier of poets. As the fifteenth century Valencian poet Ausiàs March said: *'Als naturals no par que fer se pusquen / molts dels secrets que la devdat s'estoia, / que revellats són estats a molts martres, / no tant suptils com los ignorants y aptes. / Axí primors Amor a mi revella / tals quels savents no basten a compendre, / e quant ho dic, de mos dits me desmenten, / dant aparer que folles coses parle.'* (Cançó XVIII) A brief translation might be, 'Love reveals many things that the wise fail to understand.'

And these are powerful poems, thanks to Serrano's rich and complex lexicon, to his mastery of poetic form, metaphor and diction, and to his close and meticulous attention and powers of observation, and above all to his astonishing visionary gift that makes ordinary things extraordinary. In 'Fairytale morning in Islington', the coming of day in a prosaic London

8

suburb bursts upon us like a magical happening, a symphonic overture: 'Dawn arrives with splendour / everything entrusted to dew-laden lawns / to the barking of dogs like signals / to its swarming awakening.' The poem continues to pile up riches with sensuous evocation of scents, textures, colours, but always aware of change and the passing of time.

This is a poet with an enormous curiosity for the world and our place in it, a poet who can make us feel the loneliness, as well as the power, of a circling shark, and who is always conscious of the possibility of things being otherwise, as for example in the description of trees uprooted in a great storm in 'Branches on Amhurst Road'. The drama of upended roots and branches waving in the air contrasting with the suburban street is given a voice and texture in the choice of patterns of vowel sounds. The final immobility of the tree is magically expressed in the ending stripped of verbs:

Frozen roots up in the air.
Like a net, the branches,
like a sudden flare-up.
Like arms of wind uplifted,
a crucified sky, a grapnel.

He will employ the same device with great effect in 'Frost in Auxonne' to give us an entire landscape in the grip of ice, a sonnet with only one active verb that opens the final sestet. This is a poem that fairly makes the reader ache with cold, the more so because the landscape is described in imagery relating to the human body, 'veins…fingers…spittle…breath…heart…hands'. And the body is, of course, Pedro Serrano's central image in his poetics, present in many other poems, such as 'Niño Bomba' and 'Vuelo' (Flying) which, in its musicality and harmonies, for me has echoes of 'Lustral', another love-poem from his first Arc collection, *Peatlands*. Here are the opening lines in English:

Lifted by different wings of love
I live the disparity of the elements / … /
the only scores of a multirhythmic music,
the coloratura of scattered winds,
the muffled sound of crickets…

There is so much generosity in this poet, and a vulnerability in lines like 'I want… / … / to be in the wind like the swaying of an ear of wheat/to fall into the black quagmire of trampled grapes.' In the landscapes of his poems he becomes a tutelary spirit:

> Owl-like I keep watch on the pine trees' dappled shade,
> the forsaken countryside,
> the water of the moon.

'Orfebrería' (The Jeweller's Craft), a poem of rhyming couplets, shows Serrano minutely observing, like a latter-day Jean-Henri Fabre, the movements of a dung-beetle at work, describing the creature's patience and dexterity in terms that evoke a goldsmith at work, linking the animal world with the human:

> Step by step, and little by little,
> he's gathering dung, the scarab-beetle.

> Noises he'll make, and paw the air,
> a trick well-known to the conjuror.

In 'Elípticas' (Elliptics), a moving tribute to the poet's father, a doctor, the closeness of the relationship is expressed in linguistic pairings and wordplay that borrow from scientific, medical and even astronomical lexicons. The music of the poem is antiphonal, full of echoes, an amiable conversation between father and son. Here are the opening lines:

> In a double periplus, our pupils scanning the boroughs,
> pupils both of us, my father and I, each in his time and attunement
> each keeping the other company
> in a hemispheric and helicoidal path
> along orbits that coincided that afternoon and here.

Different times and places are matched and unified to create a poem whose richness repays close reading, and goes on yielding up more and more. It also finds a kind of mirror image in a later poem, 'Diques' (Breakwaters), where the relationship being examined is the one between the poet and his two sons (though his father too is present), and it is one of the poems I most admire. With the utmost delicacy and tenderness, the poet addresses them:

> I want to go along with you and you
> on every step you take. To follow footprints

without trampling them.

That 'you and you' in Spanish is expressed in the second person singular, placing 'a ti y a ti' at the end of the first line, but in the next sentence, the poet addresses his sons using the more formal, polite form, of the third person plural and continues to do so, the last line ending with 'a ustedes.' It is as though he were teaching himself to withdraw a little, to give them space, so that it becomes a very moving rite-of-passage poem, but for the father. The last image is of playing 'ducks and drakes, with a skim and a skip – / as my father showed me and I showed both of you.' In English, of course, the distinction between intimate and polite forms of address cannot be conveyed through the pronouns, though I hope that 'both of you' perhaps conveys a slightly more formal way of speaking.

Childhood memories of a brother and sister are evoked in an astonishing, visionary poem, 'Clinamen', where they are bound into a structure both simple and complex, mirrored in the architecture of Norwich cathedral and underpinned by precise architectural terms. Examples of further transformations produced by light are explored in 'Traverseras' (Crossings), where childhood memories redeem the despoiling of landscape, restoring order and light out of man-made destruction and darkness. These poems are elemental in a very real sense, and Serrano makes us feel the redemptive power of light, water and wind, as power for change and transformation, in poems like 'Auspicios' (Auspices), 'Chopos' (Poplars), and above all, perhaps in 'Deslices' (Lapses). This poem with its close observation of walking through a snowy landscape (his native Canada), reads almost like Pedro Serrano's own poetics, where language and reality fuse and the poem speaks back to the world:

Almost only one shade,
until out of the stasis come sparks,
glints,
alliteration and merchandise,
and it's a different tune/.../
while the sun hangs, lapping,
the lingering is the path,
the gaze the act.

Anna Crowe

MADRUGADA FEÉRICA EN ISLINGTON

Amanece imponente,
depositado todo a su prado húmedo y cargado,
a sus ladridos como señales,
a su hormigueante despertar.
La ciudad amanece como siempre,
tarda en desperezarse con los primeros ruidos
y las aguas del día bañan en diferentes tandas cada barrio,
según sean los mercados o las escuelas,
las paradas del autobús o los cafés.
El día es esta decoración de la mañana,
la despaciosa entrada del calor,
del torno de la luz,
las vetas calcinadas y ocres,
el placer de un durazno allá adentro,
su rotundez de espalda,
un incipiente olor a rojo.
El día de hoy no llegó dando tumbos,
ni despertó asustado
tenso de ocupaciones y retrasos.
Discurrió lento desde la plena noche
y se fijó afirmado en el estar.
Sus horas le llegaron
como si fueran olas con basurillas
y la costra que forman hiciera la manifestación de un regocijo,
la evidencia de su llegada a la playa,
su naturalidad.

FAIRYTALE MORNING IN ISLINGTON

Dawn arrives with splendour,
everything entrusted to dew-laden lawns,
to the barking of dogs like signals,
to its swarming awakening.
The city dawns as it always does,
dawdling as it stretches with the first sounds
and the waters of day bathe each neighbourhood in turn,
whether they be the markets or the schools,
the bus-stops or the cafés.
Day is this decoration of the morning,
the lazy coming of heat,
of the turning of the light,
in burning, ochre veins,
the pleasure of a peach there inside,
with its rounded shoulder,
its rosy fragrance just beginning.
Today the day didn't come lurching in,
nor did it wake in a fright
tense with chores and delays.
Slowly it wandered in from deepest night
and stamped itself firmly on the here and now.
Its hours came to it
as though they were waves bearing litter
and the crust they form were exultation made manifest,
the evidence of its arrival at the beach,
its naturalness.

Como espigas los troncos alineados,
corales fugitivos en el bosque de niebla,
elevadas astillas y griterío,
telaraña aterida y estresada.
Las ramas negras sobre el cielo raso,
desecada toda profundidad,
garabatos y tachaduras en profusión,
arañazos en el papel gris de enero.
Contra la dura pared de cielo abierto
– un muro de cal azul e infinito cobalto –
crece la enredadera de las ramas.
Entregadas al aire se desmenuzan,
pielecilla de polvo y de durazno
quieta genuflexión hacia la tierra.
En el aire raíces congeladas.
Como una red las ramas,
como una llamarada.
Como brazos de viento levantadas,
crucifixión del cielo, garabato.

BRANCHES ON AMHURST ROAD

Like ears of wheat these tree trunks in a row,
fugitive corals in the thicket of fog,
lofty kindling and uproar,
spider's web rigid, taut with cold.
Black branches against the sky's flat roof,
all depth sucked dry,
scrawls and erasures in profusion,
scratches on January's grey paper.
Against the hard wall of open sky–
a lime wall of blue and infinite cobalt–
this bramble-knot of branches grows.
Surrendering to the air, they crumble,
flakes of dust and peach tree
a quiet kneeling earthwards.
Frozen roots up in the air.
Like a net, the branches,
like a sudden flare-up.
Like arms of wind uplifted,
a crucified sky, a grapnel.

QUEEN'S PARK

Un jardín es otro jardín y las flores desgastan
la mirada llevada suelta por el piso de tierra
– las rosas y los geranios asomándose,
los rododendros y las pragmáticas azáleas.
Un jardín es otro jardín si el aguar del alma se repitiera,
si el azúcar de un verano fuera vivo en el próximo.
Un jardín es otro jardín y ninguno sostiene,
ninguno erige un contenido,
una repercusión que no sea redundancia,
desgreñada maraña si se abandona,
hileritas inocuas si se cuida a destajo.
Espacio de ejercicios de la sombra,
esquina azul de álbumes y enciclopedias,
páramo lúcido paso tras paso perseguido
con el cuidado de quien esquiva el equívoco, el error,
de quien cada día inserta en la idea un mayor ahogo,
una despojada asfixia casi imprecisa.
Un jardín es otro jardín lleno de flores, vacío,
exhausto y traicionado en su nunca repetición.

QUEEN'S PARK

One garden is another garden and the flowers erode
the gaze carrying on unhampered by the strip of ground–
the roses and geraniums beginning to show,
the rhododendrons and the pragmatic azaleas.
One garden is another garden if the watering-down of the soul is
repeated,
if the sugary sap of one summer survives in the next one.
One garden is another garden and no one keeps it up,
no one exercises any control,
or any repercussion that is not redundant,
a tangled thicket if it is abandoned,
thin, innocuous strips if zealously cared for.
A space for exercises in shade,
a blue corner of albums and encyclopaedias,
a bright wasteland pursued step by step
with the care of one who sketches the mistake, the error,
of one who daily inserts yet more suffocation into the idea,
a rather imprecise yet stripped asphyxia.
One garden is another garden full of flowers, empty,
exhausted and betrayed in its never-to-be repeatedness.

HELADA EN AUXONNE

El campo gélido, asfixiado por una luz transfija.
Escoriados los surcos, falto de nieve todo, crispado en el ahogo.
Por los canales un brillo de venas congeladas,
dedos artríticos el filo de los árboles.
El terral un cuerpo glauco cubierto por un gel transparente.
Fosforescencia de calcio la grava,
molida por la ausencia de aire.
Una saliva metálica, un polvo helado la arada.
Emanan apenas el barro, la paja, el ramerío,
grumos ocre y marrón.
Abajo, abajo, como aliento ventral,
el valle, un cuenco de madera,
y muy adentro, el apretado corazón de un pino,
como una irradiación de manos húmedas.

FROST IN AUXONNE

The land icebound, smothered by frozen light.
The furrows abraded, no snow anywhere, but clenched and stifled.
Along the canals a sheen of frozen veins,
a ridge of trees like arthritic fingers.
Bare ground a grey-green body covered in transparent gel.
Gravel is calcium phosphorescence,
ground-down by the lack of air.
Ploughland a metallic spittle, a frozen dust.
Clay, straw, bare branches hardly emerging,
clots of brown and ochre.
Down, way down, like a deep breath,
the valley, a wooden bowl,
and far within, the squeezed heart of a pine,
like the splayed radiance of wet hands.

EL ELEFANTE DE ARQUÍMEDES

Sacude las costras terrosas y gruesas,
las ancas enormes, la falda de olanes,
levanta las patas temibles y mueve
una cola muelle.

Arroja su trompa toda una conjura,
retumba en el cielo la furia de cirros
y con un berrido desproporcionado
se lanza al pantano.

Allí, revolcando las aguas grumosas,
como si del cielo cayera ese trueno,
en la turbia mezcla de lodo y de grasas
sumerge su rabia.

La ciénaga se abre y acoge su peso,
las ondas rodean su mole furiosa
y la densa masa que el agua despliega
aquieta a la bestia.

ARCHIMEDES' ELEPHANT

It shakes its thick hide, scabby with soil,
the enormous haunches with furbelow skirts,
it lifts up fearsome feet and swings
a delicate tail.

Its trunk hurls out a great imprecation,
a rumbling in heaven of cumulus rage
and with a huge, almighty bellow
it dives in the marsh.

Churning the clotted waters there,
as though the thunder might fall from the sky,
in the turbid mixture of mud and of grease
it drowns its anger.

The swamp opens up and embraces that weight,
while waves swirl round its furious bulk
and in the dense mass that water unfolds
the creature goes quiet.

VUELO

Levantado por varias alas de amor
vivo la desproporción de los elementos,
la suavidad de sus caídas, el azoro,
las piezas únicas de una música multirrítmica,
la coloratura de vientos dispersos,
el ruido sordo de los grillos,
las risa y los ecos de corrientes diversas.
Quiero detenerme aquí y allá,
ser en el viento el gesto de la espiga de trigo,
caer en el negro lodazal de uvas apisonadas.
En medio de distintos alientos
paso una encrucijada de ramas y destinos,
la calidez del sol y el aura negra de la noche,
la piel de pan y las alas lustrales.
Vuelo no porque tema la noche de ceniza
ni el viento frío de acero despojado
sino porque las alas se abren en un punto solar,
luminarias en los polvos de agosto.
Acecho como la lechuza la parda sombra de los pinos,
el campo desolado,
el agua de la luna.
Y levanto el vuelo con la mirada en peso,
alma de amor y amor en cada ala.

FLYING

Lifted by different wings of love
I live the disparity of the elements,
the gentleness of their tumbles, the excitement,
the only scores of a multirhythmic music,
the coloratura of scattered winds,
the muffled sound of crickets,
the laughter and echoes of various currents of air.
I want to linger here and there,
to be in the wind like the swaying of an ear of wheat,
to fall into the black quagmire of trampled grapes.
In the midst of different breathings
I pass a crossroads of branches and outcomes,
the heat of the sun and the black aura of night,
skin like bread and wings washed in the light of dawn.
I fly not because I'm afraid of night with its ashes
or the wind cold as stripped steel
but because my wings open on a sunny place,
bright lights in the dusts of August.
Owl-like I keep watch on the pine trees' dappled shade,
the forsaken countryside,
the water of the moon.
And I take flight with the weight of my gaze,
soul of love and love in each wing.

LA ESPERA

La noche es solidez, estatua, viento,
columna abandonada en la ojival llanura,
profundidad abierta
en un desierto de luna en el que vaga
el alma en su desgano.
El aire, como luciérnaga fundida
al esplendor nocturno que lo anima
se hace polvo
y se acomoda en el relieve minucioso
formado por las horas.
Como si pretendiera alcanzar
la eternidad secreta
que sólo a las cosas pertenece
la noche se hace arena.

WAITING

Night is something solid, a statue, wind,
a column abandoned in the ogival plain,
deeps lying open
in a lunar landscape where the soul
in its reluctance wanders.
The air, like a molten glow-worm
in the nocturnal splendour that excites it
turns to dust
and settles into the detailed relief
shaped by the hours.
As though claiming to reach
the hidden eternity
that belongs only to things,
the night becomes sand.

HACHO

Me da terror irme con toda la sangre metida
entre la carne y el corazón,
con toda la sangre chorreando entre las heridas
sin poder contenerse,
la sangre de los otros y de los nuestros,
chopos y bergantines en un mar menor de sangre burda.
Me da terror besar la suave piel y convertirla en crimen,
buscar el alma atenta y el aterido cuerpo
y no poder tocar más que la pulpa abierta del odio,
las manos recortadas en muñones violentos,
aletas afiladas y asesinas.
Evito los brazos
para que sólo veas un muñón casi inocente y sobrio,
el rasgo rápido de la inteligencia que busca distraer de su locura
con unos cuantos golpes de timón.
Y entonces alzo los muñones como seca evidencia,
como un paso atrás, ¡detente!, no te acerques,
no veas la nata roja en que me debato y huyo,
en que me encharco para no contemplarte.
Detente entonces, digo, y bajo los ojos,
y camino así reconociendo que tampoco mis piernas
me sostienen,
que no existen o sólo con la mella que me alumbra
por encima del charco,
dos cuchillos que tambalean su propia incertidumbre,
toda esta conciencia afiebrada,
la pulpa de ecuanimidad en una gelatina congelada.
Y entonces sí,
las manitas de puerco van a salir con el calor del día.

BEACON

It terrifies me to go about with all my blood
pushed between flesh and heart,
with all that blood gushing among the wounds
unable to be contained,
the blood of others and our own,
guns and brigs in a salt lagoon of rough blood.
It terrifies me to kiss soft skin and turn it into a crime,
to search for the listening soul and the numb body
and be unable to touch more than the soft flesh of hate,
hands hacked off to violent stumps,
sharpened, murderous flippers.
I avoid arms
so you see just an almost innocent, sober stump,
the swift trace of intelligence that seeks to distract from its madness
with a few turns of the helm.
And then I lift those stumps as plain evidence,
like a step backwards, stop there! Don't come close,
don't see the blood-red morass in which I struggle and flee,
in which I paddle so as not to gaze at you.
Stop there, then, I say, and I lower my eyes,
and I walk on like that, aware that my legs
aren't holding me up either,
that they don't exist or only with the damage that lights my way
over the pool,
two knives that shake their own uncertainty,
all this feverish awareness,
the soft flesh of equanimity in a frozen jelly.
And then, yes,
the little pig's trotters are going to emerge into the heat of the day.

LUMINARIA

Como una luciérnaga en medio de un campo
hecho sólo de ruidos,
con el brillo, latente, luz adentro,
cascabel diminuto e inaudito.
Me apago hacia mí mismo para que tú te pierdas,
me apago.

LAMP

Like a glow-worm in the middle of a field
made of nothing but noises,
with the shining, intense, inward light,
minute inaudible bell.
I quench my light towards myself so that you may lose yourself,
I quench my light.

OLEAJE

Aceptar que no estás.
Dejar que pase el golpe, que se acomode,
que se instale el dolor y el desconcierto.
Aceptarlo
con la flor de la infancia en las manos abiertas.
No abrir el camarote del amor.
Aceptar que te vas
como un barco se borra
y el mar sigue.

SURGE

To accept that you are not.
To allow the blow to pass, to make space for it,
to allow grief and shock to settle in.
To accept it
with the flower of childhood in your open hands.
Not opening love's cabin.
To accept that you're going
the way a boat grows fainter
and the sea carries on.

BRISA

Como no hay realidad dependo ahora
entre tú y yo del ruido de las hojas,
de las señales de los muertos,
de la vibración tenue del alma.
Como no hay realidad tú vas y vienes
como el viento, que está y desaparece.
Hace mucho que no te cuento nada.
¿Quién soy? ¿Quién eres tú sin mí?
No sé describir el desacomodo, el seguimiento.
Queda restituir, si se puede, una coloración de cristal.
Quiero la suavidad, el agua quiero,
que se deposite físicamente en paz
que algo se encienda en ti y en mí,
como un viento que besa.

BREEZE

Since nothing is real I depend now
between you and me on the sound of the leaves,
on the signals made by the dead,
on the frail vibration of the soul.
Since nothing is real you come and go
like the wind, that is here and then vanishes.
For a long time now I've told you nothing.
Who am I? Who are you without me?
I can't describe the awkwardness, what follows.
We still need to restore, if possible, a tinting of glass.
I want gentleness, I want water
physically, peacefully, to pour down
so that something may catch fire in you and in me,
like a wind that kisses.

LA MAR OCÉANO

Quieto, reducido a la inequidad de un teatro vacío
solapado rastra la lenta majestad del mar.
Relamida, suave, disconforme,
una humedad salivosa se pega siempre a quien se acerca.
Se le ven las costillas en cada ramalazo,
apenas tres hileras de lomo liso, fluctuante.
Como los dientes.
De repente de nada sale un grito,
el gesto maquinal y obcecado,
el santo olor de la sangre.
Chac, chac, chac.
La furia fría del escualo, su seda,
la boca rápida en la lustrosidad del agua.
Chac, chac, chac, se sacude.
En el océano interminable y solo el pez da vueltas.

Reduced to the iniquity of an empty theatre, calmly,
warily, it trawls the slow majesty of the sea.
Gloating, smooth, inimical,
a mucus-like saliva always sticks to whatever comes close.
With every lash of its tail the ribs can be seen,
barely three rows of smooth flank, rippling.
Like the teeth.
A cry, suddenly, out of nowhere,
the stubborn, mechanical expression,
the blessed smell of blood.
Chac, chac, chac.
The cold fury of the shark, its smoothness,
the swift mouth in the lustrous water.
Chac, chac, chac, it shakes itself.
In the endless, lonely ocean the fish goes on circling.

NIÑO BOMBA

El niño se lleva la mano al diente,
duda.
Las bombas
no le han explotado.
Todo su cuerpo
se sacude
y no sabe
si se tiene que quitar
el calzoncillo.
No puede enseñar
su diminuta e inerme
creencia en sí.
No se sabe ante las cámaras,
tampoco lo piensa.
¿Qué
puede pensar el niño?
Volver
a ser un cuerpo mondo,
un temblor,
un gesto mínimo
que la cámara aprieta
como un aceite de paz.
Todos somos
esa gana de vida.
Oración
en un vacío
alrededor del mal.
Un gesto que es de todos,
el pudor infantil,
el cuerpo desnudo
que quiere conservarse
y crecer.
Así,

CHILD BOMB

The boy lifts a hand to his tooth,
in doubt.
The bombs have not blown him up.
His entire body
shakes
and he doesn't know
if he should remove
his underpants.
He cannot show
his tiny and defenceless
belief in himself.
He doesn't know he is in front of the cameras
nor does he even think about it.
What
can the boy think?
Go back
to being a plain body,
a trembling,
a slight gesture
which the camera fastens on
like an oil of peace.
We are all
this hunger for life.
Prayer
in a void
around evil.
A gesture which is everyone's,
a childish shame,
the naked body
that wants to preserve itself
and grow.
And so,

esa visión del niño
como un aceite lento
nos abarca.
Hay que correr
a protegerlo,
sacarlo de esa escena,
paralizado de horror.
Lo que no pasó.
Ahora el niño
y sus vigilantes
y nosotros
somos ese aceite,
ese calor oleaginoso
y obligatorio.

Este poema lo escribí hace unos años, al ver en la televisión la noticia de un niño palestino en la frontera con Israel. En el último momento el niño se arrepintió, y en lugar de hacerse estallar con las bombas que le envolvían el cuerpo, se entregó. Esa era la noticia. Lo que se veía era mucho más. Muchas vidas, entre ellas la suya, por ese gesto a la vez airoso y heroico, se salvaron. Lo publico en estos momentos en que está pasando tanta muerte, mucha de ella infantil e innecesaria.

Tiempo después me encontré con un ensayo de James Fenton en la New York Review of Books *(https://www.nybooks.com/ articles/2018/07/19/sculpture-bodies-spitting-image/) en el que menciona una escultura del artista iraní Reza Aramesh. Cuando leí su descripción, "An Israeli soldier points his gun at the Palestinian youth asked to strip down as he stands at a military checkpoint along the separation barrier at the entrance of Bethlehem, March 2006", no tuve duda, incluso antes de ver la pieza en internet, de que su origen era el mismo y conmovedor video que yo había visto años atrás. Lamento la urgente vigencia de lo que este poema trata de invocar.*

this vision of the child's
like a slow oil
wraps itself round us.
We must make haste
to protect it,
remove it from this scene,
paralysed with horror.
That which did not happen.
Now the child
and his guards
and ourselves
are that oil,
that oily and necessary
warmth.

I began this poem some years ago, after seeing on television the news item about a Palestinian boy on the Israeli frontier. At the last minute the boy repented, and instead of blowing himself up with the bombs strapped to his body, he gave himself up. That was the news item. What we saw was much more. Many lives, his own among them, were saved through this gesture, at once graceful and heroic. I publish this at this time when there is so much death happening, much of it the deaths of children and unnecessary.

Some time later, I came upon an essay by James Fenton in the New York Review of Books *(https://www.nybooks.com/ articles/2018/07/19/sculpture-bodies-spitting-image/) in which he mentions a sculpture by the Iranian artist, Reza Aramesh. When I read the description, "An Israeli soldier points his gun at the Palestinian youth asked to strip down as he stands at a military checkpoint along the separation barrier at the entrance to Bethlehem, March 2006", I had no doubt, even before I saw the sculpture on the internet, that its origin was the identical and moving video I had seen years before. I deplore the present and lamentable relevance of what this poem attempts to convey.*

ORFEBRERÍA

Pieza a pieza, paso a paso,
junta la caca el escarabajo.

Hace ruidos y se agita,
rueda que rueda el ilusionista.

Por la cal y el terregal
a pie juntillas intenta arar.

Nada hay que no le sirva,
paja, cerillos, sal y lascivia.

Al final, en tornasol,
bate y alza esta perla marrón.

THE JEWELLER'S CRAFT

Step by step, and little by little,
he's gathering dung, the scarab-beetle.

Noises he'll make, and paw the air,
a trick well-known to the conjurer.

Over lime and dusty ground
with feet together he tries to plough.

There is nothing that cannot be used,
straw, spent matches, salt and lust.

Finally, like beaten gold,
he hammers, lifts high this rich brown globe.

ELÍPTICAS

En un periplo doble, pupilas oteando barrios,
pupilos mi padre y yo cada uno en su tiempo y acomodo
acompañándonos mutuamente
en hemisférico y helicoidal recorrido
de órbitas coincidentes esa tarde y aquí.
Cruzamos sin novedad el Shepherd Bush, vasculando
hacia el laboratorio de un colega suyo,
yo qué sé de testigo de sí mismo en su busca,
doblando embudos, técnicas, buriles,
tácitos vasos de precipitado, matraces de la vida,
matracas en aras de ambos rumbos.
De ahí a pie juntillas regresamos
de mi infancia al momento
justo, como siluetas en juego doble y solitario,
en acabadas perspectivas puntuales, en canasta.
¿Qué recorríamos? Requeríamos
simplicidad, capacidad pulmonar, zancos, zancudos.
Íbamos garzas reales de aquí para allá,
en la maroma padre e hijo
dando la vuelta de regreso a Bloomsbury.
Aquí, dijo, viví, en esta esquina de Tottenham Court Road
por la que yo tanto pasaba, coincidental y ajeno.
Siguiendo al tú por tú inigualables
en constreñida imagen, consternada
conversación pudiente,
grácil en su paseo, calma granjeada.
Irrepetibles, si no fuera por eso, tales cuitas, grajeas
desperdigadas por las escaleras del University College,
añicos en el polvo solar
cruzando descubrimientos
rodando estelares.

In a double periplus, our pupils scanning the boroughs,
pupils both of us, my father and I, each in his time and attunement
each keeping the other company
in a hemispheric and helicoidal path
along orbits that coincided that afternoon and here.
We cross Shepherd's Bush without mishap, oscillating
and arterial, making for the laboratory of one of his colleagues,
with me as, who knows, maybe a witness to that visit,
cutting corners on glass funnels, technologies, flasks,
tacit jars of precipitate, retorts holding life,
their rattle acknowledging both environments.
From there we come back in step with each other
from my childhood to just the right moment
like silhouettes in a game for two, or in solitaire,
or punctually finished perspectives, a canasta.
What were we surveying? What we pursued
was a simple life, ease of breath, stilts, long-legged mosquitoes.
We stalked, regal as herons, from here to there,
along the tightrope-of-father-and-son
taking the homeward path to Bloomsbury.
Here, he said, is where I lived, on this corner of Tottenham
                                                    Court Road
past which I so often walked, coincidental and foreign.
Following that equilibrium that cannot be replicated
in a constrained environment, came fraught
yet flowing conversation,
graceful in its strolling, its well-earned calm.
Never to be repeated, were it not for that, so painstaking, like pills
or marbles sent spinning down the staircase of University College,
random fragments in the solar dust
cutting across discoveries
travelling like stars.

En compañía de ambos trazos, brazo con brazo
distintas metas robustecidas
—¿para quién si no las marigolds?—,
la compañía paterna y filial en su equinoccio cada uno
de por sí merecidos y mecidos
en el regazo de amor que nos llevaba
cada uno en su órbita.

Companionable in the paths of each, arm in arm
different goals now strengthened –
for whom if not the marigolds? –
the company of father and son each in his equinox
through his own merits and lulled
in the lap of love that bore us
each one in his orbit.

AUSPICIOS

Pujando de oro el cielo,
a la presión convidado,
un cuervo como un crayón negro posa
su vuelo en la arista de un álamo,
extendiendo ramas, abarcando
ese cuadro por él constituido.
Reclinando la luz,
haciéndola girar en escalones
por las frondosidades y el follaje,
altisonante observa,
desmedido,
y de repente calla.
Es así que un aviso allí está
para que en sí crepite
y el árbol bulla entonces en luz, hierva
una lluvia cayendo en sí de sí como en Pissarro,
estallando meticulosamente,
intensa y en callada,
en verde de dorada.
En ese instante todo es puro augurio:
la escuela, el canto, el árbol,
protegiendo la vida allí depositándose
para que crezca y viaje en sí
en un plano apaisado, en cortinaje
de fondos verdes y de luz alterna,
dejándome a mi propio albedrío,
y el cuervo un tachón en un aviso suave,
y todo ya de nuevo auspicio.

OMENS

The sky straining into gold,
ushered in to pressure,
a crow like a black crayon settles
his flight on a poplar's brim,
spreading branches apart, embracing
this picture that he has created.
The light now reclining,
he makes it spiral into a staircase
through leaves' fronds and foliage,
with strident observations,
overweening,
and suddenly falls silent.
It's therefore a sign that's there,
so as to crackle in itself,
and the tree rioting then in light, that rain
boils falling into itself out of itself as in a Pissarro,
exploding meticulously,
intense, untold,
to green from gold.
In that moment all is pure prediction:
the school, the singing, the tree,
protecting the life being laid down there
so that it may grow and travel by itself
in a treescape of level, pied horizons,
green depths that alternate with light,
leaving me to my own impulse,
and the crow a footnote to a gentle message,
with everything now become omen once again.

DIQUES

Yo quiero acompañarte a ti y a ti
en cada paso. Seguir las huellas
sin pisarlas, verlos
cruzar de playa en playa alzando surcos
allí donde plantaron la inhalación,
donde se fueren en cabriolas.
Todo vacío ha de llenarse de nuevo
suavemente diría, de sí, de sus anhelos,
sin disolverlos ni colmarlos.
Ser en la sombra un hueco cálido
en el cual acogerse si la ocasión lo pinta
o lo despintan los vaivenes.
Ser quien salpique de alientos
su propio guarecerse
para no intimidar ni incomodar
y que de nuevo puedan las olivas
llenar el plato común de la concordia.
Ser el agua que se recoge en una curva
del río haciendo playa
en la que los guijarros salten de costado
y hagan patitos, chip, chip,
como mi padre me enseñó y yo a ustedes.

BREAKWATERS

I want to go along with you and you
on every step you take. To follow footprints
without trampling them, to see you
crossing beach after beach, making tracks
there where you planted an in-breath,
or where you vanished into cartwheels.
Everything empty is replenished
gently, I'd say, from itself, from your longings,
without dissolving or filling them to the brim.
To be a warm hollow in the shade
in which to take refuge if the need arises
or if comings and goings spoil it.
To be one who sprinkles with his breaths
his own sheltering
so as not to intimidate or trouble
and so that the olives may once more
fill the common dish of harmony.
To be the water that gathers at a bend
in the river creating a beach
where the pebbles may skip sideways –
ducks and drakes, with a skim and a skip –
as my father showed me and I showed both of you.

A cada ras de metro de banqueta,
nos encontrábamos, gracias
a su comedimiento y gentileza
y al barrunto de sal de su hosquedad
en un florecimiento hecho de pautas
fijas y a la ligera. Dos o tres conocidos anclaron al principio
la tensión de las velas y así zarpamos.
Después ya casi todo iría viento en popa.
Salir a navegar cada diez días
para ver qué atrapábamos
en el océano de la conversación.
Me recogía en mi casa en Kilburn,
y hacíamos el trayecto en su coche
como un prólogo acordado.
Dos candeleros puestos en Hampstead nos hacían compañía.
Fuimos en contingencia pertinaces.
Compartíamos una pinta y una segunda más,
que religiosamente él las pagaba.
Después, sin abandonar el salvavidas del vaso,
mi parte en la amistad, dos medias yo pedía,
y así nos íbamos, dando que te dando.
Sin nervadura ni provecho, yo, sin ton ni son,
me retrasaba cada tarde entre el salir y no salir,
en un revoloteo.
Un acarreo de anclas de angustia
como algas varadas en la playa
me impedía avanzar, pegado el viento a mis frutos adentro,
soliviantado en la violencia,
mientras él esperaba. Y así salía,
regresando siempre al pie de la noche
contento, satisfecho,
a continuar mis días de cubrecama y a cubierto.
De pestañas y de fibras y de uñas está hecha la amistad.
De la argamasa dúctil de miopías y persistencia.

I'd shuffle to the kerbside like an awkward Tube traveller,
and there we'd meet, thanks
to his courtesy and kindness
and to a twinkle of salt in his grimness
in a blossoming made of habits
both fixed and relaxed. Two or three acquaintances at first
kept the sails taut and so we cast off.
Afterwards we almost always had the wind behind us.
We'd go out for a sail every ten days or so
to see what we could catch
in conversation's ocean.
He would pick me up from my house in Kilburn,
and we would do the journey in his car
like a pre-arranged agreement.
Two ship's lights, lit in Hampstead, accompanied us.
Regarding contingencies, we were thorough.
We shared a pint, and then another,
which he would religiously pay for.
Afterwards, without letting go of the lifebuoy of the glass,
my part in the friendship, I would ask for two halves,
and so we'd go on, turn and turn about.
With no ribbing or profit, without rhyme or reason,
I would hesitate every evening, over whether to go out or not,
havering endlessly.
A hauling of anchors of anguish
like sea-wrack stranded on the beach
prevented me from advancing, as though I'd eaten a rotten apple,
my guts violently stirred up,
while he was waiting. And like this I would go out,
always coming back at the end of the night
happy and satisfied,
to continue my daytime existence as a bedspread and hidden away.
Friendship is made up of eyelashes, fibres, fingernails.
From the malleable mortar of short-sightedness and persistence.

Una chamarra alta y unas manos en los bolsillos
en espera, allí siguen. Luego el viaje hacia el pub
y la dorada blonda espuma de la cerveza
amarga hasta la dulzura y el daguerrotipo.
Me siento a ver con él el mar en el Masnou
como si fuera Brighton.
Desde allí oteamos estos espacios abiertos,
los humaderos de los pubs, sobreseídos
en el esfuerzo de uno y otro por entender de qué se trata
el estar aquí, en esta vida

A collar-up jacket and hands-in-pockets
are waiting, already there. Later the trek to the pub
and the golden blond froth on the beer,
bitter merging with sweetness and the daguerrotype.
I sit down with him to gaze at the sea at El Masnou
as though it were Brighton.
From there we scan these open spaces,
the smokehouses of pubs, dismissed
in the attempt by each of us to understand what it means
to be here, in this life.

LA HABITACIÓN AZUL

Si afuera sólo fuera
el correntín del día viajero
de su nombre a la infancia.
Si afuera acostumbrara
el cielo a despertar archisonante,
chirriante a veces.
Si afuera esas ventanas pintadas en azul
llegaran a caerse o a quejarse.
Si afuera en lo que fuera le llegara,
quieta en su viaje a la quietud,
los tiestos en expectativa,
las cajoneras mismas,
sus resguardos.
Si afuera sólo fuera
tocando tras de sí lo que se queda,
las manos de los nietos en sus manos,
la habitación en lo que se deserta.
En el acanalado los ángulos del cuarto,
en el tapete azul los zapatos atentos y en desuso,
la despedida cierta.

THE BLUE ROOM

If outside there were only
the breeze of the wandering day
blowing from her name back to her childhood.
If outside the sky might only grow accustomed
to waking up resonant with song,
chirruping, sometimes.
If outside those windows painted in blue
might come to collapse or complain.
If outside whatever might be there might reach her,
lying quiet on her journey into quietness,
the flower-pots waiting,
even the chests-of-drawers
with their treasure.
If out there she could only
be reaching backwards to what remains,
the grandchildren's hands in her hands,
the room in what is left behind.
In the grooved mouldings the room's four corners,
on the blue rug the watchful slippers no longer needed,
the goodbye certain.

TRAVERSERAS

There will be a tunnel and light
ANNE CARSON

Cuando tenía ocho años
un túnel atravesaba la carretera de terracería,
que años después sería asfaltada.
Paso del agua en lluvias y de arañas en secas,
yo y mis hermanas atravesábamos
rumbo al resplandor del otro lado
una travesía apenas penumbra
de sombras benévolas y aleteos.
Arriba, por esa carretera atravesaron luego
camiones de redilas de la batida secreta
en contra de la guerrilla de Atoyac.
Atravesaron también años después
camiones y camiones con troncos de la tala,
los cuerpos recostados bajados de la sierra.
Más adelante dejaron unos bultos,
cuerpos arrumbados del narco,
un pastoreo anónimo en una guerra anémica.
Apenas ayer las dos bocas del túnel las tapiaron
con restos de basura abandonados
como quien no quiere la cosa.
En el tapiado ahora siembran milpas
esmirriadas que apenas sobreviven.
Todo eso se lo van a llevar las primeras crecidas
y unos niños correrán por el túnel de luz
de felicidad en felicidad en atrabancada travesura
y todo volverá a sorprender
sin dejar rastros ni restos ni vestigios.

CROSSINGS

There will be a tunnel and light
ANNE CARSON

When I was eight years old
a tunnel ran under the gravel road
that years later would be tarmacked.
A path for water when it rained and for spiders when dry,
my sisters and I would go through it
towards the brightness at the far end,
a barely twilit crossing
of kindly shadows and flutterings.
Overhead, along this highway flatbed trucks crossed later on,
used in the clandestine hunting down
of Atoyac guerrilla fighters.
Years later, too, lorry after lorry
would cross with trees from the logging,
felled bodies being brought down from the mountains.
Later there were abandoned bundles,
ruined bodies from the narcotics trade,
anonymous shepherding in an anaemic war.
Only yesterday the two mouths of the tunnel were walled up
with remains of abandoned refuse
scattered quite casually.
In the walling-up they're now sowing sweetcorn,
spindly plants that barely flourish.
The first heavy rains will carry all this away
and children will charge through the tunnel of light
from joy to joy, crossing pell-mell,
and everything will once again astonish
without leaving rubbish or remains or any trace.

CLINAMEN

En el artesonado de la catedral de Norwich,
elevándose hasta lo infinito,
una curva lleva a otra que lleva a otra
en un oleaje ingobernable,
voluta por voluta.
Y en el cielo del cielo las nubes,
querubines y orejas y pies,
con los ojos y el cuerpo y los ángeles
dando vueltas convulsas.
No sé cuándo empezamos a ser
parte ni cuando la ola
girará sin nadie que la siga.
Pero ahora vamos
en una punta del ala mi hermano
y yo en la otra como gran regocijo,
viento en popa, olfateando
esa playa de hornos y sanguijuelas
en que nos bañábamos.
Y mi hermana María vuela también,
allá en lontananza,
en la rueda de la fortuna en que viajamos,
porque hoy es su cumpleaños.
Porque hoy se cumplen en una sola arista
todas esas curvas y estrías de la madera,
y crecen hacia lo alto por pliegues y pilares,
y se alzan en olas dando vueltas, piruetas,
disparadas al techo, iluminándonos.
Y el tiempo resta sobre su propio peso,
se acomoda en la piedra que lo contiene
y todo vuelve a seguir su curso
en un lento, iluminado clinamen.
Allá arriba, desde ese vértice,
disparándose en todas direcciones.

CLINAMEN

In the vaulted roof of Norwich cathedral,
soaring up into the infinite,
one curve lifts another that lifts another
in an ungovernable surge,
volute upon volute.
And in the sky of heaven the clouds,
cherubim and ears and feet
with eyes and the body and the angels
convulsively revolving.
I don't know just when we begin to be
part of it nor whether the surging wave
will swerve with no one to follow it.
But here we go,
my brother at one wing tip
and I at the other like a great rejoicing,
wind astern, sniffing
that beach of leeches and furnaces
where we used to swim.
And my sister María flies as well,
there in the distance,
in the wheel of fortune on which we travel,
because today is her birthday.
Because today there come together in a single arris
all those curves and timber flutings,
and they multiply upwards in folds and columns,
and rise in waves, revolving, pirouetting,
shooting up into the roof, shedding light on us.
And time remains firm upon its own weight,
adapting itself to the stone that holds it
and everything returns to its usual groove
in a slow, illumined clinamen.
Shooting away in all directions
from that apex high above.

CHOPOS

Alzados,
subiendo por sí mismos
talla verde en el azul,
arañando enredaderas de aire.
Cada uno su propia alzadura
cabellos al viento,
su propia plegaria.
Surgen de la masa más verde,
articulándose,
mechas de voluntad en el espacio.
Quietos, altivos,
concentrados en su apogeo
parpadeando de luz, inmateriales casi.
Tiemblan de miedo,
cada hoja, cada rama,
crines hirsutas, verticales.
Comendadores de dios, poetas
de la displicencia o el cansancio,
pinceles del azul, panteras verdes.
Recortados al agua, casi reflejos,
tótemes de cristal.

BLACK POPLARS

Towering,
rising all by themselves,
a green carved out of blue,
clawing at creepers of air.
Each one its own hoisting,
hair in the wind,
its own litany.
They emerge from the greenest mass,
uttering themselves,
wilful fuses in space.
Calm, proud,
centred on their crowns,
glittering with light, incorporeal, almost.
They tremble with fear,
each leaf, each branch,
a thick, upstanding mane.
God's ancient knights, poets
of indifference or weariness,
brush-strokes of blue, green jaguars.
Cut-outs in water, virtual reflections,
totems of glass.

DESLICES

Detenido suavizado
en la felpa y lo blanco,
en su hálito estático,
en la pendiente,
en lo que se acumula
de las cosas:
la rajadura, las ramas,
lo quebradizo.

Todo inclinado hacia sí mismo,
sosteniendo
en vertical y paralelo y oblicuo
la nieve,
puesta ahí a descansar.

En el entramado del pino,
en su bordado alto,
en la rueca ruda del tronco,
en el tocón,
la paz de los alimentos
de la tierra, lo entretenido,
que aquí se toca apenas,
apunta.

Casi sólo un matiz,
hasta que de la estasis saca chispas,
brillos,
aliteraciones y mercancía,
y es otro el cantar.

Mientras tanto,
mientras eso sucede,
mientras el sol cuelga y lame,
la detención es el camino,

LAPSES

Held back, softening
in the plush and the whiteness,
in its ecstatic exhalation,
on the slope,
in what piles up
out of things:
the splinterings, the branches,
brittleness.

Everything leaning towards itself,
bearing,
vertical and horizontal and oblique
the snow,
put there to rest.

In the pine's timber framework,
in its lofty embroidery,
in the trunk's rough distaff,
in the stump,
the peace of the earth's
supports, what is maintained,
which here barely comes into contact,
strikes home.

Almost only one shade,
until out of the stasis come sparks,
glints,
alliterations and merchandise,
and it's a different tune.

All the while,
while this is happening,
while the sun hangs, lapping,
the lingering is the path,

la mirada el acto.
El entrever un entrevero,
en la ramada.

Porque la huella de la huella
apenas sale a flote,
deja rastro, apura,
cae en su propio peso
la sensación y el abandono,
el desasimiento
desmoronándose
en donde estoy.

La nieve
con su vellón solapa todo,
afelpa las acciones,
tapa lo recóndito, lo por apurar,
la cascada crispada y sonora con que rompe
la nueva estación.

Baja entonces el agua en chorro entero,
cuando se abre el hueco, destapa
la corriente, el hoyo negro en plural,
lo inconsiderado.

Debajo de tanta calma el río sigue.
En el hueco se ve su corrección,
su alivio.
Dando tumbos se desentraña
la tierra, lo recóndito, lo necesario.
Abajo el limo ferviente, el nacimiento
del agua, los parabienes.

Mantengamos la calma. Hagamos
de la nieve un estandarte, potencia,
actividad recóndita.
Alcemos en la espera del polvo blanco
el resguardo de lo que acontece,
su protección.

the gaze the act.
A glimpsing, an intermingling
among the branches.

Because the footprint of the footprint
barely floats free,
leaves a trace, takes fright
sensation and abandonment,
fall back in their own weight
the detachment
crumbling away
here where I stand.

The snow
haps everything in its fleece,
velveting actions,
seals up what's hidden, to be feared,
the clenched and sonorous waterfall with which
the new season breaks in.

The water then comes down in a solid gush,
when the hollow is opened, it unseals
the current, the hollow black and plural
the overlooked.

Beneath so much calmness the river continues.
In the breach it sees its own correction,
its relief.
Somersaulting, the soil, the recondite, the needful
is disembowelled.
Below is the fervent clay, the birth
of water, the congratulations.

We need to keep calm. We should make
of snow a banner, a potency,
a hidden activity.
While we wait for this white dust, let's raise
the defence of what happens,
its protection.

Bajemos poco a poco la ladera,
sin desbarrancar, hacia el silbo.
Acotemos.

Se desliza la calma
por una superficie de esporas
que en lenta aparición protege, cubre,
deja caer, acontece.

Let's make our way slowly down the hillside,
without falling over the edge, towards the whistle.
Let's get closer.

Calm glides
over a surface of spores
that in its slow appearance protects, covers,
lets fall, happens.

PEDROO SERRANO is a poet and translator born in 1957 in Montreal, Canada. He studied at the University of Mexico (UNAM) and at Kings College, University of London (KCL). He founded the Avispero-Festival de Poesía de Chilpancingo in the South of Mexico and directed the Banff International Literary Translation Centre in Canada's Rockies. He teaches Poetry and Translation at UNAM.

He has published eight books of poems in Spanish, and English translations of his poems have appeared in several anthologies and magazines in Britain, Canada and the USA. Arc published his collection *Peatlands* in 2014, translated by Anna Crowe and introduced by W. N. Herbert.

The bilingual anthology of contemporary British and Irish poets, *La generación del cordero* (The Lamb Generation) that he co-translated and co-edited with Carlos López Beltrán, was for Simon Armitage "one of the most interesting pieces about the whole movement". He has also translated into Spanish William Shakespeare's King John, Gabriel. A Poem by Edward Hirsch and Figure in a Landscape by Anna Crowe.

His 'Canciones lunáticas' (Lunatic Songs, music by Hilda Paredes) were performed by the Arditti Quartet at the Wigmore Hall in London in 2011, and the collaborative exhibition Camouflages, done with the Austrian painter Johanes Zechner is to be exhibited in 2025 in Graz, Madrid and Mexico City.

Pedro Serrano was awarded a Guggenheim Poetry Fellowship in 2007 and the Prix International de Poésie Antonio Viccaro in 2016.

ANNA CROWE, poet and translator, was born in England in 1945, read French and Spanish at the University of St Andrews, and has lived in Fife since 1986. In 1998, with Brian Johnstone and Dr Gavin Bowd, she founded StAnza, Scotland's International Poetry Festival.

She is the author of four full poetry collections, the third of which, *Not on the Side of the Gods* was published by Arc in 2019, and three chapbooks, of which *Figure in a Landscape* (Mariscat 2006) received the Callum MacDonald Memorial Award, was a Poetry Book Society Choice, and brought her a residency at the Harvard Summer School in 2011. Her poetry has been recorded for the Poetry Archive, anthologised, and translated into Catalan, Castilian, German, Italian and Galician.

As a translator, she has received Poetry Book Society Recommended Translation awards for *Tugs in the Fog*, (Bloodaxe 2006), translations of the work of the late Catalan poet, Joan Margarit, and *Maps of Desire* by the Catalan poet Manuel Forcano (Arc, 2019). For Arc she translated the anthology *Six Catalan Poets* (2013), *Lunarium* by the Catalan poet Josep Luis Aguilo (2016), and *Peatlands* (2018) by the Mexican poet Pedro Serrano..